GRAPHIC LIBRARY

JACKIE ROBINSON

Takes the Field

by **Elliott Smith**

illustrated by **János Orbán**

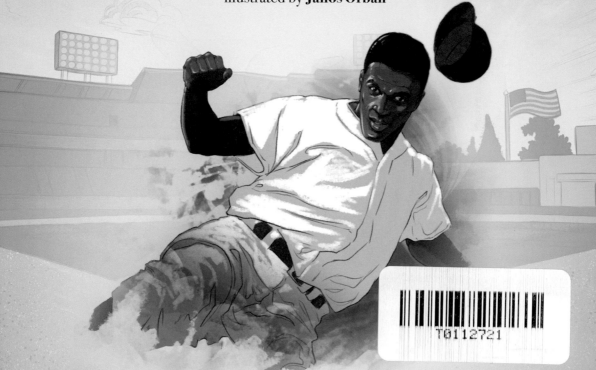

CAPSTONE PRESS
a capstone imprint

Published by Capstone Press, an imprint of Capstone
1710 Roe Crest Drive, North Mankato, Minnesota 56003
capstonepub.com

Library of Congress Cataloging-in-Publication Data
Names: Smith, Elliott, 1976– author. | Orbán, János, illustrator.
Title: Jackie Robinson takes the field / by Elliott Smith ; illustrated by János Orbán.
Description: North Mankato, Minnesota : Capstone Press, [2024] | Series: Great moments in history | Includes bibliographical references. |Audience: Ages 8 to 11 | Audience: Grades 4–6 | Summary: "On April 15, 1947, Jackie Robinson made history when he stepped onto the baseball diamond as a Brooklyn Dodger. For the first time in more than 60 years, a Black player took the field in a professional baseball game. How did Robinson break through the racist barriers that had kept so many Black athletes out of professional sports? And what is the enduring legacy of his remarkable accomplishment? Find out in an easy-to-read graphic novel that reveals why Jackie Robinson's shattering of the color barrier in baseball is among the greatest moments in history"—Provided by publisher.
Identifiers: LCCN 2022047884 (print) | LCCN 2022047885 (ebook) | ISBN 9781669016892 (hardcover) | ISBN 9781669016847 (paperback) | ISBN 9781669016854 (pdf) | ISBN 9781669016878 (kindle edition) | ISBN9781669016885 (epub)
Subjects: LCSH: Robinson, Jackie, 1919–1972—Juvenile literature. | Baseball—United States—History—20th century—Juvenile literature. | Discrimination in sports—United States—History—20th century—Juvenile literature. | African American baseball players—Biography—Juvenile literature. | Baseball players—United States—Biography—Juvenile literature. | LCGFT: Biographical comics. | Graphic novels.
Classification: LCC GV865.R6 S6355 2024 (print) | LCC GV865.R6 (ebook) | DDC 796.357092 [B]—dc23/eng/20221013
LC record available at https://lccn.loc.gov/2022047884
LC ebook record available at https://lccn.loc.gov/2022047885

Editorial Credits
Editor: Christopher Harbo; Designer: Tracy Davies; Production Specialist: Katy LaVigne

Design Element by Shutterstock/kzww

Cover art by Charles Stewart III

All internet sites appearing in back matter were available and accurate when this book was sent to press.

Direct quotations appear in bold italicized text on the following pages:

Page 19 (middle), from "Did You See Jackie Robinson Hit that Ball?" by Woodrow Buddy Johnson and Count Basie (Baseball Almanac, February 2023).
Page 19 (bottom), from *The Jackie Robinson Story* (Eagle-Lion Films, 1950).
Page 20, from "The Story Behind Jackie Robinson's Moving Testimony Before the House Un-American Activities Committee" by Eric Nusbaum (*TIME*, March 24, 2020).
Page 25, from "Jackie Robinson's Final Public Appearance: 50 Years Ago at 1972 World Series" by Rhiannon Walker (*The Athletic*, October 21, 2022).

Printed and bound in China 5379

TABLE OF CONTENTS

Jackie Robinson was a natural-born athlete.

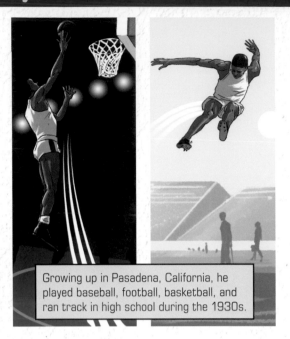

Growing up in Pasadena, California, he played baseball, football, basketball, and ran track in high school during the 1930s.

Robinson excelled at all four sports and continued to play them at Pasadena Junior College. He even ran track alongside his brother Mack before switching to the University of California, Los Angeles (UCLA) in 1939.

Robinson's experiences as an athlete were unique. He attended integrated schools in California, which was unusual because many Black and white students went to separate schools at that time.

Let's see if you can beat me, little brother.

I'm going to give it my best shot!

At UCLA, Robinson was one of four Black players on the most integrated major college football team in the country.

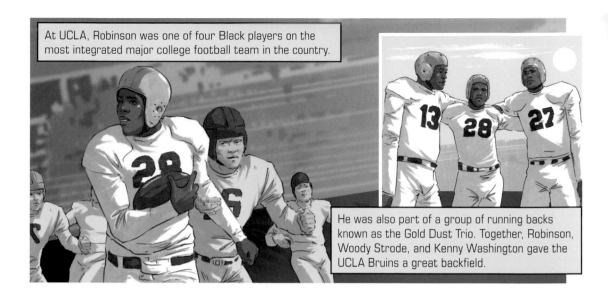

He was also part of a group of running backs known as the Gold Dust Trio. Together, Robinson, Woody Strode, and Kenny Washington gave the UCLA Bruins a great backfield.

Robinson also played major roles on UCLA's basketball and track teams. He is still the only athlete in UCLA history to earn a varsity letter in four sports.

Surprisingly, baseball was Robinson's weakest sport at UCLA. In 1940, he had a low batting average—just .097!

The team relied on his speed and defense. But few would have guessed that Robinson would someday be one of the most important players in Major League Baseball (MLB) history.

After college, Robinson spent some time playing semi-pro football in Los Angeles and Hawaii.

Two days after he left the islands to return to Los Angeles, the Japanese attacked Pearl Harbor, Hawaii, on December 7, 1941.

The surprise attack thrust the United States into World War II (1939–1945), and it soon changed the direction of Robinson's life as well.

In 1942, Robinson was drafted into the U.S. Army. He was assigned to a segregated unit at Fort Riley in Kansas.

With the help of boxing champion Joe Louis, Robinson was admitted to Officers Candidate School (OCS). After graduating OCS, he was named a second lieutenant.

Life in the army was difficult for Black soldiers. They dealt with poor facilities, unclean bathrooms, limited transportation options, and verbal abuse from fellow soldiers and officers.

What do you want, Robinson?

We need more seats on the bus, sir. The men have to be able to travel around the base.

We'll see, soldier.

As an officer, Robinson pushed for better conditions for Black soldiers. After meeting with resistance, he had some success improving the facilities.

But progress was slow, and Robinson faced setbacks. In July 1944, he was riding on an army bus in Texas when . . .

Get to the back of the bus!

There is no more segregation on an army post. I can sit here!

Robinson refused to move, citing a recent ruling that military buses were no longer segregated. But he was charged with insubordination and court-martialed. After a trial the next month, he was cleared of all charges.

Then Robinson was sent to Camp Breckinridge in Kentucky. He stayed there as a coach for various army sports teams until his honorable discharge in November 1944.

After leaving the military, Robinson served as the basketball coach for Samuel Huston College in Austin, Texas, for one season.

C'mon, fellas, let's run the fast break!

At the same time, he started thinking about professional sports.

But segregation limited his opportunities. In 1945, no professional sports league allowed Black players.

And when it came to pro baseball, Black players had been excluded for decades. Not since Moses Fleetwood Walker, a catcher in the mid-1880s, had a Black player taken the field.

Why? Because the MLB owners came to a "gentlemen's agreement" that banned Black players in 1887.

With no other place to play, the Negro Leagues helped fill the void for Black baseball players starting in 1920. Originally made up of eight teams, the Negro Leagues were home to some of the world's best baseball players. And fans loved the action.

Legends like Cool Papa Bell, Josh Gibson, and Satchel Paige played in the Negro Leagues.

Negro Leagues baseball was just as good as—and in some ways better than—the major leagues. And it soon proved instrumental in bringing Robinson back to the game he loved.

In 1945, Robinson made his way back to baseball by trying out and winning a spot with the Kansas City Monarchs.

Congratulations, Jackie. You made the team.

Thanks! You won't regret having me.

The Monarchs were one of the best teams in the Negro Leagues.

Starting out, Robinson was a little rusty. The 26-year-old hadn't played baseball in several years, and the travel schedule in the Negro Leagues was grueling.

But that didn't stop him from making an impact. In 34 games, Robinson had an excellent batting average of .375, including four home runs and 13 doubles.

During his year in the Negro Leagues, Robinson also had a couple of important sidetracks. In April 1945, he and two other Black players traveled to Boston for a tryout with the Red Sox.

This tryout isn't real. They don't want me.

Even though Robinson performed well, the tryout was for show only. The Red Sox, known for a culture of racism, had no intention of signing a Black player.

But another meeting proved much more fruitful. In August, Robinson traveled to New York to meet Brooklyn Dodgers general manager Branch Rickey. Rickey was eager to break baseball's color line. And he had just the right person in mind.

Do you have the courage to play the game no matter what happens? I'm looking for a player with the guts to NOT fight back.

I can do it. It will be hard, but I can.

Rickey signed Robinson to a minor league contract. He would play the 1946 season for the Montreal Royals.

Robinson became the first Black player in the minors since the 1880s.

And he loved his season in Canada. The fans welcomed the second baseman and his new wife, Rachel.

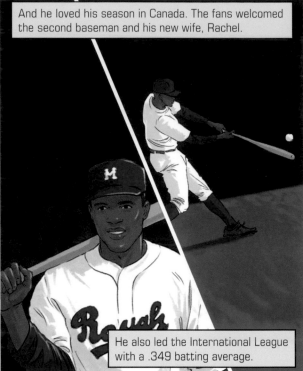

He also led the International League with a .349 batting average.

By the end of the season, Robinson helped the Royals win a hard-fought Junior World Series against the Louisville Colonels.

After the 2–0 win in Game 6, cheering fans mobbed Robinson and carried him off the field.

In 1947, Robinson returned to spring training as a member of the Royals.

But based on his great performance in 1946, it seemed clear he would be moving up to the majors with a spot on the Brooklyn Dodgers roster.

However, several Dodgers players passed around a petition against Robinson joining the team. Dodgers manager Leo Durocher quickly set his players straight.

Listen, I don't care if he's white, Black, or green--if I say he plays, he plays!

On April 10, 1947, Robinson officially signed a contract with the Dodgers. Five days later, he made his debut on Opening Day in Brooklyn.

A crowd of more than 26,000 people watched the game at Ebbets Field.

In terms of baseball stats, April 15 was not a day to remember. Robinson played first base and went hitless in four at-bats. His biggest highlight was reaching base on an error and eventually scoring the game-winning run.

But in the pages of history, April 15 was a moment to remember. Robinson became the first Black player since Moses Fleetwood Walker to play major league baseball.

Robinson's first season in the majors wasn't easy. He faced racist chants from the stands, some fans threw objects at him, and opposing players cursed his name.

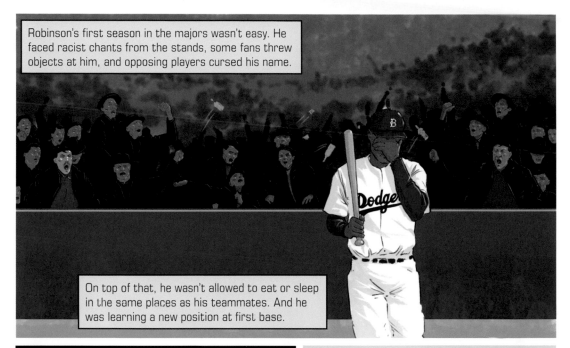

On top of that, he wasn't allowed to eat or sleep in the same places as his teammates. And he was learning a new position at first base.

One of the worst incidents happened in a game against the Philadelphia Phillies. That team's manager told his players to swear and shout racial slurs each time Robinson came up to hit.

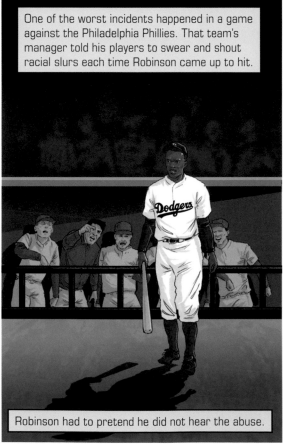

Robinson had to pretend he did not hear the abuse.

He was supposed to handle it all in silence. One of the reasons why Robinson was selected to break the color line was his promise to stay calm.

But inside, Robinson burned with anger. He often felt as if he was alone on an island, not on a baseball diamond with his team.

Robinson's closest ally was newspaper reporter Wendell Smith. Smith wrote for the *Pittsburgh Courier*, the largest Black newspaper of the time.

Branch Rickey hired Smith to travel with Robinson while writing his columns. He often served as Robinson's roommate on the road.

I don't think I can take it anymore, Wendell. It's hard out there.

Ignore the hecklers. You've got to keep fighting. You're setting an example for so many people.

Robinson's rookie year was filled with memorable moments. But many were ignored by the media, and some may have been invented. One popular story is that Dodgers infielder Pee Wee Reese draped his arm around Robinson to quiet hecklers in Cincinnati.

While it makes for a nice story of friendship, no one is sure if it ever happened.

And—while he and Reese did become great friends over the years—Robinson was on his own more often than not during his first season.

Despite the ups and downs, Robinson's rookie season ended on a high note. He finished with a .297 batting average, 12 home runs, and 48 runs batted in (RBIs). He also was named the first-ever Rookie of the Year.

In all, it was a remarkable season. While facing immense pressure and awful racism, Robinson earned the respect of his teammates and became a key member of the Dodgers.

In 1948, Robinson moved to his natural position of second base during his second season. With one year under his belt and a more familiar place on the diamond, he excelled.

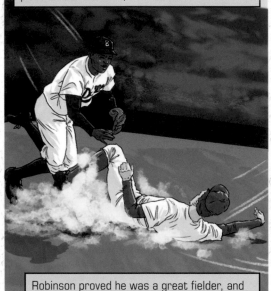

Robinson proved he was a great fielder, and his batting average remained steady at .296.

More importantly, Robinson had opened a door to the majors for other Black players. Soon after Robinson, Larry Doby joined Cleveland's roster and Hank Thompson and Willard Brown joined the St. Louis roster.

Welcome to the bigs, Larry.

Thanks, Jackie, for everything you've done.

Robinson was no longer the sole focal point for breaking the color barrier.

After the 1948 season, Robinson spent the offseason working on his hitting—and it really paid off. His third season was the best year of his career. He hit .342 with 124 RBIs. Plus, he was a terror on the base paths, with 37 stolen bases.

Robinson was also named the starting second baseman at the All-Star Game—the first All-Star Game to include Black players.

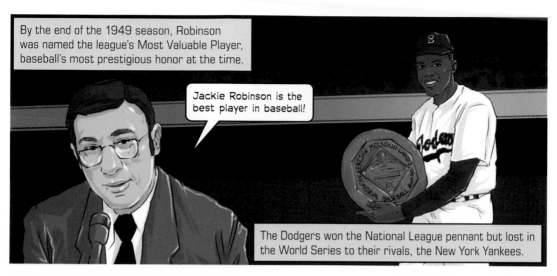

By the end of the 1949 season, Robinson was named the league's Most Valuable Player, baseball's most prestigious honor at the time.

Jackie Robinson is the best player in baseball!

The Dodgers won the National League pennant but lost in the World Series to their rivals, the New York Yankees.

After that banner year, Robinson's popularity skyrocketed.

Did you see Jackie Robinson hit that ball?

MY OWN STORY

He spent his offseason speaking to audiences across the country. His autobiography, *Jackie Robinson: My Own Story*, was a success, and he was even the subject of a hit song on the radio.

Robinson also starred in *The Jackie Robinson Story*, a 1950 movie about his life.

Yes, this is the Jackie Robinson story. But it is not his story alone. Not his victory alone. It is one that each of us shares.

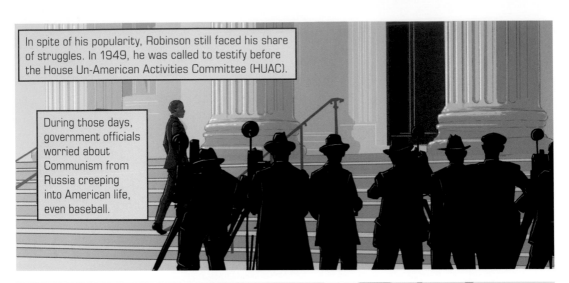

In spite of his popularity, Robinson still faced his share of struggles. In 1949, he was called to testify before the House Un-American Activities Committee (HUAC).

During those days, government officials worried about Communism from Russia creeping into American life, even baseball.

Robinson denied Communism, but he took the opportunity to speak out against racism.

[Black people] were stirred up long before there was a Communist Party, and they'll stay stirred up long after the party has disappeared unless Jim Crow has disappeared by then, as well.

Back on the field, Robinson and the Dodgers put together a string of winning seasons. In 1951, the Dodgers made the playoffs but lost the National League pennant to the New York Giants.

And in 1952 and 1953, the Dodgers made it to the World Series—only to lose to the Yankees both times.

Great game, Jackie. We almost had 'em.

We've got to figure out a way to beat the Yankees. I'm not going to have many more opportunities.

By 1954, Robinson was 35 years old. He was no longer the Dodgers' starting second baseman. He began playing a variety of positions around the diamond and in the outfield.

And even though he played fewer games in 1955, Robinson still accomplished one of his biggest goals. The Dodgers overcame the Yankees and won the World Series.

We did it!

Robinson was finally a world champion!

Robinson played one more season with the Dodgers. But then the unthinkable happened. On December 13, 1956, the Dodgers traded Robinson to their biggest rival, the New York Giants.

However, Robinson never suited up for the Giants. About a month after the trade, he told the Giants that he would be hanging up his cleats for good.

Jackie finished his 10-year career with a .311 average. He was a six-time All-Star, and he led the Dodgers to the World Series six times. But numbers alone hardly do his career justice.

By the time Robinson retired, it was common for MLB teams to have Black players on their rosters. Superstars such as Willie Mays, Ernie Banks, and Satchel Paige were among a growing number of Black players in the league.

With his baseball career behind him, Robinson turned his attention to the business world. He went to work for the Chock Full O'Nuts coffee company—serving as the first Black vice-president in a major U.S. company.

He also remained a powerful voice for change within baseball and society. He fought for Civil Rights, walking alongside thousands of people at the March on Washington in 1963.

Thanks for coming, Mr. Robinson!

I wouldn't have missed it for the world.

In 1962, Robinson became eligible for the Baseball Hall of Fame. He urged voters to consider his on-field play, not his cultural legacy, and he was elected on the first ballot.

It's the greatest honor any person could have.

JACK ROOSEVELT ROBINSON

Robinson kept a low profile in retirement. Diagnosed with diabetes, he spent many years struggling with his health.

In one of his final appearances, he threw out the first pitch before Game 2 of the 1972 World Series.

Then he thanked the crowd and delivered a message as only Robinson could do.

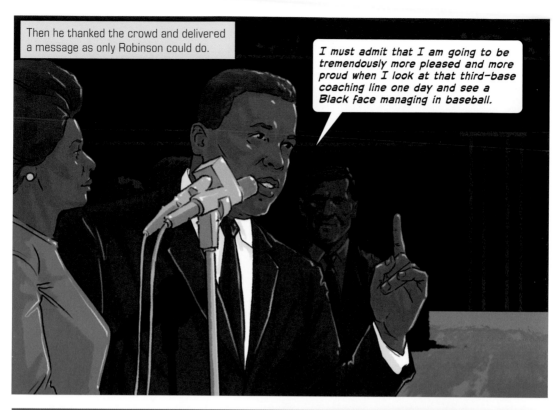

I must admit that I am going to be tremendously more pleased and more proud when I look at that third-base coaching line one day and see a Black face managing in baseball.

Nine days later, on October 24, 1972, Robinson passed away. He was just 53 years old.

In the history of sports, few players stand as tall as Jackie Robinson. His courage in the face of horrific racism inspired the larger Civil Rights movement. Dr. Martin Luther King Jr. once said Robinson was "a legend and a symbol in his own time."

After his death, Robinson was awarded both the Presidential Medal of Freedom and the Congressional Gold Medal, two of the nation's highest honors.

Robinson has also been honored many times by baseball. In 1997, his number 42 was retired across the league.

Every April 15—the same day he broke the color barrier—all MLB players and managers wear Robinson's number 42.

And the Los Angeles Dodgers feature a statue of Robinson sliding into base outside of their stadium.

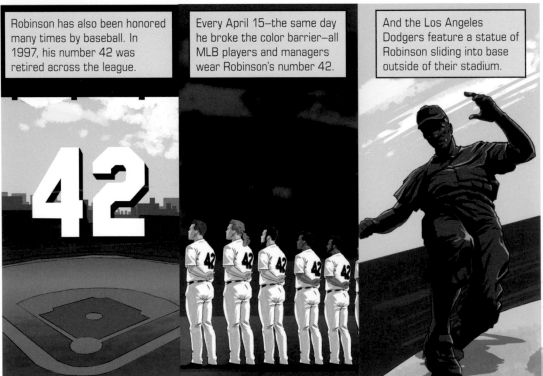

For all his awards and honors, perhaps the thing that would make Robinson most proud is what happened two years after his death. In 1974, Cleveland named Frank Robinson (no relation) its manager, making him the first Black person to hold that position. Since then, other Black managers have followed, including Dave Roberts with the L.A. Dodgers.

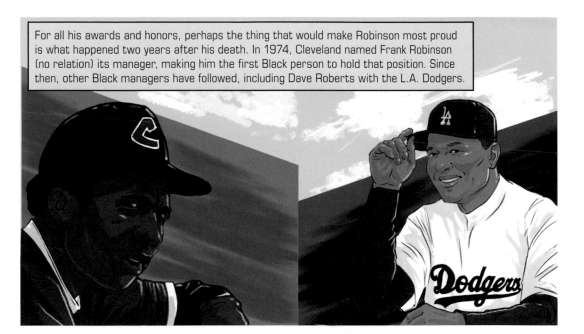

Even though Jackie Robinson is a towering figure in sports, he mostly wanted to be remembered as a player who gave the game his all. He shouldn't have had to face adversity in the first place. But he did. And he helped change sports for good.

As Robinson once said, "I'm not concerned with your liking or disliking me . . . all I ask is that you respect me as a human being."

MORE ABOUT
JACKIE ROBINSON

- At UCLA, Robinson twice led the Pacific Coast Conference
  (later known as the Pac-10) in scoring in basketball,
  became the NCAA champion in 1940 in the broad jump
  (25 feet, 6.5 inches), and achieved All-American status
  in football.

- Robinson's brother Mack won the silver medal behind Jesse
  Owens in the 200-meter race in the 1936 Berlin Olympics.

- After college, Robinson was hired to play semi-pro football
  with the Honolulu Bears. Their first exhibition game was
  in Pearl Harbor, Hawaii. He left Honolulu on December 5,
  1941, just two days before the Japanese attacked.

- On August 29, 1948, Robinson hit for the natural reverse
  cycle against the Saint Louis Cardinals. This means
  Robinson's at-bats, in order, were: home run, triple,
  double, single. Only nine other players have accomplished
  this feat.

- In 1957, Robinson, along with Martin Luther King Jr., received an honorary Doctor of Law degree from Howard University.

- Although Robinson broke the color line, he wasn't the first Black player to win a World Series. Larry Doby and Satchel Paige earned championships in 1948.

- Robinson's number 42 was retired by the Dodgers alongside Roy Campanella's 39 and Sandy Koufax's 32 in 1972.

- In 1982, Robinson became the first baseball player featured on a U.S. postage stamp.

GLOSSARY

batting average (BAT-ting AV-rij)—a measure of how often a player gets a hit in baseball

communism (KAHM-yuh-ni-zuhm)—a way of organizing a country so that all the land, houses, and factories belong to the government, and the profits are shared by all

court-martialed (KORT-mar-shuhld)—tried as a member of the military for being accused of breaking rules or committing a crime

diabetes (dy-uh-BEE-teez)—a disease in which there is too much sugar in the blood

drafted (DRAFT-ed)—to be selected to serve in the military

heckler (HEK-luhr)—a person who shouts rude comments at a performer or a sports player

insubordination (in-sub-or-duh-NAY-shuhn)—refusing to obey orders

integrated (IN-tuh-grate-uhd)—accepting of all races

minor league (MYE-nur LEEG)—a group of teams where players improve their playing skills before joining a major league team

pennant (PEN-uhnt)—a triangular flag that symbolizes a league championship

petition (puh-TISH-uhn)—a letter signed by many people asking leaders to change something

resistance (ri-ZISS-tuhnss)—an opposing force

rookie (RUK-ee)—a player who is playing their first year on a team

roster (ROSS-tur)—a list of players on a team

segregated (SEG-ruh-gay-ted)—separated by race

READ MORE

Hudak, Heather C. *Jackie Robinson.* Minneapolis: Kids Core, 2020.

Nash, Sibylla. *Athletes for Racial Equality: Jackie Robinson, Arthur Ashe, and More.* North Mankato, MN: Capstone, 2022.

Williams, Yohuru, and Michael G. Long. *Call Him Jack: The Story of Jackie Robinson, Black Freedom Fighter.* New York: Farrar Straus and Giroux Books for Young Readers, 2022.

INTERNET SITES

Los Angeles Dodgers: Jackie Robinson Timeline 1919–1949
mlb.com/dodgers/history/jackie-robinson/timeline-1919

National Baseball Hall of Fame: Jackie Robinson
baseballhall.org/hall-of-famers/robinson-jackie

Society for American Baseball Research: Jackie Robinson 75
sabr.org/jackie75

ABOUT THE AUTHOR

Elliott Smith has written more than 40 chapter books for young readers on a variety of topics. He previously worked as a sports reporter for newspapers. He lives in Falls Church, Virginia, with his wife and two children. He loves reading, watching sports, going to concerts, and adding to his collection of Pittsburgh Steelers memorabilia.

Photo by Elliott Smith

ABOUT THE ILLUSTRATOR

János Orbán grew up in Budapest, Hungary, where his love of art began at an early age. After graduating from an art high school, he went on to earn a degree from the Hungarian University of Fine Arts. With a passion for illustration, Orbán most enjoys designing characters and creating artwork for children's books. He has two daughters and a son, and currently lives and works with his family in a village near Budapest.

Photo by János Orbán